# There's a Hole

# in My Sidewalk

## THE ROMANCE OF SELF-DISCOVERY

# Portia Nelson

**ATRIA** PAPERBACK
New York London Toronto Sydney New Delhi

BEYOND WORDS
Portland, Oregon

**ATRIA**
PAPERBACK

A Division of Simon & Schuster, Inc.
1230 Avenue of the Americas
New York, NY 10020

**BEYOND WORDS**
1750 S.W. Skyline Blvd., Suite 20
Portland, Oregon 97221-2543
503-531-8700 / 503-531-8773 fax
www.beyondword.com

Copyright © 2012 by Portia Nelson
Originally published by Popular Library © 1977, ISBN 0-445-03199-9
Previously published by Stonebarn © 1988, ISBN 978-0-96211-590-5
and by Beyond Words Publishing © 1993, ISBN 978-0-94183-187-1

Managing editor: Lindsay S. Brown
Design: Devon Smith

First Atria Books/Beyond Words paperback edition October 2018

**ATRIA** PAPERBACK and colophon are trademarks of Simon & Schuster, Inc.
**BEYOND WORDS** PUBLISHING and colophon are registered trademarks of Beyond Words Publishing. Beyond Words is an imprint of Simon & Schuster, Inc.

For more information about special discounts for bulk purchases, please contact Simon & Schuster Special Sales at 1-866-506-1949 or business@simonandschuster.com.

The Simon & Schuster Speakers Bureau can bring authors to your live event.
For more information or to book an event, contact the Simon & Schuster Speakers Bureau at 1-866-248-3049 or visit our website at www.simonspeakers.com.

Manufactured in the United States of America

10 9 8 7 6 5 4 3 2 1

*The Library of Congress has cataloged the 1993 edition as follows:*

Nelson, Portia.
  There's a hole in my sidewalk: the romance of self-discovery / by Portia Nelson.
       p.   cm.
Originally published: Los Angeles; Popular Library, 1977.
1. Self-realization. 2. Self-perception. 3. Maturation (Psychology). 1. Title.
BF637.S4N45 1993
158'.1—DC20

                                                    93-18380

ISBN: 978-1-58270-685-6
ISBN: 978-1-4516-8635-7 (ebook)

The corporate mission of Beyond Words Publishing, Inc.: *Inspire to Integrity*

"I am part of all
that I have met."
—TENNYSON

To all of you,
whoever you are,
I humbly dedicate this book.

## PERSONAL NOTE

I choose to call these thoughts "pieces"... pieces of me. These pieces have had a bit of trouble finding a comfortable concept that would knit them into one book... just as I have had difficulty molding a multi-faceted misfit into one person.

More than anything, they are evidence, to me, that here in the middle of my life I have finally gained a small pin-point of self-awareness... false images stripped away... "through a glass darkly, but, now... face to face." No hiding, anymore, behind innocence and ignorance.

It isn't necessarily easier now... but I have a self that I trust and feelings and the experience are mine... not what I should feel... not what I was taught to feel and not something someone else felt that I admired and imitated. Knowing one's own feelings and being able to trust them is the difference between existing and living. So, that's what I have here, I guess... living and loving experiences... pieces of my small universe that can, I hope, be recognized by yours.

# EDITOR'S NOTE

I am pleased to present the 35th Anniversary Edition of *There's a Hole in My Sidewalk*. This extraordinary book was originally published in 1977, and since then it has become a well-loved classic. The humor, inspiration, insight, and comfort found within these pages have touched thousands of people. *There's a Hole in My Sidewalk* is not just another book that sits on the shelf; it is a trusted friend people turn to time and again. I am thrilled to be reissuing a book that has offered so many people hope and inspiration.

The opening poem, "Autobiography in Five Short Chapters," has been quoted in more than two hundred books. This simple, elegant poem depicts a universal journey that is at once deeply human and unwaveringly straightforward, and has helped guide many on their own path to self-discovery. If you are familiar with only this poem, I think you will be delighted to read the entire work.

Portia Nelson's writing is a clear, honest depiction of self-reflection, inner conflict, personal struggle, and, ultimately, resilience, personal growth, and hope, which has resonated deeply with those making transitions in their lives. *There's a Hole in My Sidewalk* has been especially significant to those recovering from addiction, as well as their loved ones, and has been used in many 12-step and recovery programs. As the publisher of this book, Beyond Words is honored to contribute to this tradition.

In the late 1990s, I had the pleasure of spending time with Portia Nelson in New York where she lived at the time. What a lovely woman she was! Portia led an accomplished life and left us with an impressive legacy that spans an acting career, which includes her role in the classic movie *The Sound of Music*, her body of work as a singer and composer, which includes five solo albums on major labels, and her work as writer, a result of which you now have in your hands. Although Portia is no longer with us, she is here in spirit, speaking to our hearts from the pages ahead.

I am proud to help continue Portia's legacy with this special edition. To celebrate this milestone we are releasing the book in hardcover for the first time, thus creating an enduring package to hold this timeless classic. I know that this book will continue to have great meaning in numerous lives for many more years to come. My hope is that one of those lives will be yours.

Cynthia Black
President and Editor in Chief
Beyond Words Publishing

# CONTENTS

**A** story of
ME in You
and
You in Me
in
Five Short Chapters

## PROLOGUE

My life has been a series
of wonderful experiences.
It's a pity I wasn't there
for most of them.

# AUTOBIOGRAPHY IN FIVE SHORT CHAPTERS

## Chapter One

I walk down the street.
> There is a deep hole in the sidewalk.
> I fall in.
> I am lost....I am helpless.
>> It isn't my fault.
It takes forever to find a way out.


## Chapter Two

I walk down the same street.
> There is a deep hole in the sidewalk.
> I pretend I don't see it.
> I fall in again.
I can't believe I am in this same place.
>> But, it isn't my fault.
It still takes a long time to get out.

### Chapter Three

I walk down the same street.
There is a deep hole in the sidewalk.
I see it is there.
I still fall in...it's a habit...but,
my eyes are open.
I know where I am.
It is *my* fault.
I get out immediately.

### Chapter Four

I walk down the same street.
There is a deep hole in the sidewalk.
I walk around it.

### Chapter Five

I walk down another street.

# CHAPTER ONE

**I** don't know what I want sometimes,
But I know
that I want to know
what I want.
I know that once I know what I want
I will be able to get it.
Of course, I may not want what I get
when I get it....
But, at least
I'll know I don't want that!
Then, I can move on to something else
I don't know if I want.
That's progress!

You say you love me for who I am....
But...
who you think I am
is not *who* I am.

Therefore,
it's hard for me to be who I am
when we're together...

because...
I think I have to be
who you think I am.

Of course,
I don't know exactly who it is
you think I am...
I just know it isn't who I am.

Who am I?
Well...
Who I am is something I recognize
when someone tells me
who I am *not*.
At least, I *think* that's *not* who I am.
Maybe who I am *not*
is who I *am*!
If that's who I am... MY GAWD...
you really love me.

I used to suffer a great deal
thinking I was the only one
   in the world
   so lonely
   and troubled.

Then, I opened the door to myself
and discovered there were
   millions
   of people
   just like me.

It isn't lonely anymore...
but it's miserable to be
   so ordinary.

**I** know why we are friends.
It's because I don't always
                approve of you.

You don't think you deserve approval.
So… if I gave it to you,
                you would not
                approve of me
and I would lose your trust.

Friendship is based on trust
                and I want you
                to trust me
because I need your approval.

However, if I get your approval,
                I will not trust you
because I don't think I deserve approval
                either.

I know why we are friends.

**Y**ou want to please me... and,

I want to please you...

> so please make the decision
> about where we are going tonight.

If I make the decision...
> and then *you* don't like it,
> you'll be mad at me
> and I'll be miserable all evening
> because I haven't pleased you.

Now... if *you* try to please me...
> and *you* make the decision,
> and I don't like it
> when we get there...
> at least *you* will be pleased.

If I am unhappy with where we are,
> or what we are doing,
> that alright...

because it won't be my decision
that will have made you unhappy.
> It will be yours.
> Therefore,
> it will be *your* fault!
> > *That* will please me.

You say you will never leave me
        because I understand you.
And I love being thought of
        as "understanding."

But, I also understand
        that by being so understanding,
        you automatically
        have the freedom
        to do as you please...
        because...
if I am not understanding,
        you will leave me.

I think that what I really
        have to understand is this:
In order to be so understanding all the time
        (so that you will not leave me),
        I have to leave myself.

If I am not myself
      when I am being so understanding,
      who the hell is it
      you will never leave?

Better I should not be so understanding
      so there's somebody
      you can leave.

**Y**ou have made a fool of me!

I know that I am not the most beautiful,
the most talented, the most intelligent
            person in the world...
            but I liked you...
            and I wanted you
            to think I was.
So... I tried to be beautiful
            talented and intelligent
            for you.

However,
            since I succeeded
            in making you believe it,
naturally,
            I immediately
            lost respect for you
            for not seeing
            that I had fooled you.

Now...
            I am intelligent enough,
            beautiful enough and
            talented enough

not to be associated with fools...
and I am incensed that I didn't see
      how foolish you were
          at once.

But...
      I liked you then... and...
it drove me to make you believe
      what I wanted you to believe....

Except...
      I was so convincing,
      I began to believe it myself!

Now...
      anybody who believes
      things like that about me
         is a fool.

That makes me a fool!

And if it weren't for you
      believing what I wanted you to believe,
      I wouldn't know that.

I hate you for making a fool of me!

**W**ill you please stop trying to
        finish my sentences before I do?

It's humiliating!

After all… it's my sentence!
        Let me show it off!

I know you are really trying to let me know
        how sensitive and smart you are…
        and how deeply you understand me….

But… if you are that smart…
        please let me think that
        I am smarter than you
        by not impressing me with
        how smart you are
        in the middle of my sentences!

Of course,
>   if I am smart enough
>   to be aware of
>   what you are up to…

Then,
>   I should be smart enough to know
>   it doesn't matter what you do
>   in the middle of my sentences.

Maybe I'm not so smart!

Now, that *is* humiliating!

I want you to love me...
>> but I am aware
>> that you only love
>> what you cannot get.
>> So, I can't let you know
>> that I am interested
>> or you won't love me back.

Now...
>> I hate games
>> and dishonesty
>> more than anything.

Therefore...
>> if I love you enough
>> to be dishonest...
>> to play a game
>> in order to keep you interested,
>>> I will hate myself.
>> If I hate myself,
>>> eventually,
>>> I will crack up!

If I crack up…
    at least,
    you won't be able to get me…
        because I won't care…
        or be aware
        that you even exist…
    and then,
    maybe you will love me.

Jesus! There's got to be a simpler way!

**Y**ou are strong... vital...
            very much in control of yourself.
I admire that!
I know you can help me...
            and I need help.

But,

            if I allow you to help me,
            I will have to trust you enough
            to give up my own self control.

If I give that up,
            I will begin to feel powerless...
            without identity...
            like a nobody!

How dare you help me to be a nobody!

**I** cannot seem to leave you…
       though often,
       I think I should because
       even though I care…
I am not in love with you.
But I am in love with the fact
       that you are in love with me.
It makes me think very well of myself,
When I think well of myself,
       I am very nice…
       and very creative.
That makes me feel worthwhile and then
       I love myself.
The more I love myself…
       the more you love me.
No wonder I can't leave.
       I wouldn't know
       I loved myself…
       without you.

I would like to be one...
A one not worried about being two!
I am more one
           when we are three.
When we are two,
           I become a zero.
I become zero because
I am afraid you will see
           that I am not one.
When we are three, I am comfortable...
It doesn't matter if I am not one
           since I seem to become one
           simply because
           there are two being two
           and letting me be one.
Therefore, I am not zero... I can't be...
Two from there is always one.
So, I am more one when we are three...
           as long as I don't worry about
                      being two.

In the beginning
  everywhere I went,
  I didn't always go along.
I didn't know it then,
  but I was afraid I'd meet myself
When we finally met,
I wasn't who I expected I'd be…
  but, oh, it was a relief
  to have someone to be with…
  at last.

# CHAPTER TWO

I am a hopeless romantic
        who does not believe
        love solves everything.
Still, I weep for the loss
                of illusion…
        knowing full well
                that reality
        is unbearable…
without a few gilded window frames
                to see through.

**H**ow brazen you are!

You lean across the table...
        slender hands
        cupping your face...

and stare arrow-straight
        into my eyes...
        no blinking at all.

You know you are making a frame

for a remarkably beautiful face.

I stare back...
        not out of desire
        or challenge...

        but as my only defense
        against your discovering

how deeply I am immersed in pleasure.

I hope that what you are after
is an exchange…
not
a reaction.

One step forward
        into the bright of loving.
Yet, I fear the bright will not last.
        … so, one step back.
Still, I fear more,
        the dark of not loving at all.
Well then…
        may I take a giant step?
        May I?
I have already answered.
        Shall we dance?

I know who you are.

You are so much of me
       that if I don't love you
       I won't exist.

And I'm selfish.
       I don't want to miss anything.

**T**wo days ago
I never would have believed
I would spring from my bed
        at the first glimmer
                of sunlight…
and drive all over town
        looking for
        blue Volkswagens!

**D**ear one…

Kind one…

>	lend me your dreams
>	for a while.

Cover me
>	with the sweet sleep
>	of your innocence,
and wake me
>	with the crystal sunshine
>	of your hope.

Light my darkness with fireflies
>	and build me air castles
>	to house
>	the velvet summers
>	of love.

Stay with me,
>	dear one…
stay with me long enough
>	to let me hear again,
>	that far away music
>	of yesterday…
>		when I was young.

Your hair is like a monk's cap
        made of wheat.

It often slips down over your eyes
        so I can't see if you are
        hiding from me
        or spying on me.

Sometimes
        I reach out...
        as an artist might...
and make a gentle brush stroke
        on the canvas of your brow
        to change the shape of your cap.

As much as I love it,
I cannot bear to talk to you
        without watching your eyes.

Besides,
        there is such selfish pleasure
        in the act of touching,
        lightly...
        hardly at all...
making a graceful arc there
and seeing you smile...
        as if your hair were attached
        to the corners of your mouth.

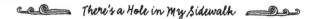 

There is so much about me that I don't know
until I talk to you.

That first day...
　　　　　　as you turned to leave...
　　　　　　we touched...
and, like magnets, we clung to one another
　　　　　　for a long time.
　　　　　　Nothing more.
Yet...in that rare moment of holding you
I experienced what I have come to value most...
　　　　　　the ecstasy
　　　　　　of
　　　　　　not doing anything
　　　　　　about it.

**H**ow wise of you to wait...
to fill the shy, awkward spaces
    with white wine
    and cushioned conversation.
I am aware that you are
    allowing me time
    to become accustomed
to the cities of your smile...
and to window shop your eyes...
    until, at last,
    I am so full of you,
that I no longer blush
    on my way into your arms.

Water, Air, Earth, Fire.

Mix together slowly,
                with ceiling seagulls
                and pear wine.

Stir until the perfect blend…

Cool for a moment…then,
                place in the fruitful womb
                of love
                to be born again
                into a circle of light…

an enchanted world where only believers
                are allowed to enter.

I can feel my fear beginning
             to settle inside me…
             like sleepy kittens
             upon the hearth
Shshshsh…tip toe…
Don't slam doors in my mind…
             not now.
Let the kittens sleep a little while
             please…
The fire will die soon enough, anyway…
And now, while the world is warm…
             hold me.

**I** think I just fell into a hole
in the sidewalk.

I have said, "I love you"…
> before you,
> and meant it.

Yet,
I would have to admit…
> that laid on the scales,
> the pain of loving
> has often outweighed the joy.

But, it never ceases to amaze me
> that I never died of love.

Looking back…
> knowing I survived…
> pain has become my faith.

Though I am fragile…
> it is my strength.

So, I warn you…
> I will not die of you.

I know that pain and joy
      cannot be separated…
      and, like tomorrow and today
      they become one another.

And so, I remember those
      before you,
and rejoice that I said,
      "I love you"
      before you…

because,
it will help me not to die of you…
      like I didn't
      before you.

I am always a grumbling sleepwalker
in the mornings.

Do you realize…
for three days in a row
I have laughed
at least ten times
before coffee?

It's a dreary day....
Let's just stay inside.
We can pretend that
     Kisses are brushes
     and that we are
     each other's canvases.
We won't need a northern light...
     or any light at all,
     for that matter....
And who cares if we ever finish
     the picture, anyway.

Sorry I didn't answer.
I was listening
        to what you weren't saying.

You are the oldest young person
                    I have ever known.
It makes me feel younger than you are.
                    That's a neat trick!

**I** am so free with you,
I never wish to be
       free of you.

The beautiful togetherness
      of our silence
      makes me wonder
why we ever bothered
      to speak at all.

**I** didn't really
      leave my heart
      in San Francisco…
although I said I did….
But, I certainly
      let it out
      into the fresh
           morning air
and ran it up and down
           a few hills.
I did let it rest
      in the smile
of a beautiful stranger
      for a few days…
But then,
      I snatched it away
      and brought it home
           to you…
as I knew I would
      before I went away
      to be mad at you.

I think I love you most
in those early hours
just before sunrise
When,
spent with loving
and lost in dreaming,
You reach out,
like the morning glory vine,
and wind about,
braiding limb to limb,
binding me to you
with the tender quiet
of us.
Desire is buried in slumber...
and,
asking nothing...
giving all...
You bend to touch me
through a thousand years of knowing
...without knowing.
But I know.
I'm glad I'm a light sleeper.

When I listen
    to your feelings,
    and can feel
    your listenings…
Only then
    can I expect you
    to hear me.

**W**e are not "in love"…
but, we are love.
I'm glad.
It lasts longer.

**M**y longing is burning a hole
      in my patience....
      Time is spinning away.
What good is sleep
      when an eternity
      is rushing by
      that I could be kissing you?

Damn it!
Will you please wake up?
I think I'll turn over...
      a little bump
      never hurt anybody!
"Hey!...awake so early?
      I love you."

**P**lease understand…
There are days I must leave you…
    in order to be closer to you.
Up close, I cannot search out
    those fragments of you
    that your image of yourself
    hides from me.
At a distance…
    uncluttered be sensation…
    I can really see you, freely…
    and discover pieces of myself,
        as well.
And then, we come home together…
    to love you all the more.

You said you didn't love me
                    this morning.
I didn't believe you.
I knew you just hated yourself.
                    That's alright.
I don't love you either...
                    today.

**P**lease…
don't extract promises from me
that must race quickly
        from the present
        into the past
casting dark shadows on the future.
Now…today…is all
        we can be certain of
        and love
        is something better
than a collection of pretty vows
to cling to on a rainy day.
What we already are
        *is* what we will be
                together.
        Isn't that enough?

**S**top looking at me like that!
Can't you see how much
    I need you to believe
    what I am saying
so that I can believe it
        myself?

I would give you everything…
                    if I could…but,
the only gift worth giving
                    is freedom…
the freedom to grow…
                    away from me
                    if necessary.
Of course, one can't give freedom,
but, at least I know that.
Maybe that's the gift then…
                    the knowing….
And I couldn't tie a ribbon around it
                    even if I wanted to.

**A**sk something of me...
                please.
I know there is no answer...
                but often,
I need to feel it would be me
                you would ask...
if there was one.

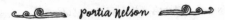 

I am not locking out!
I am trying very hard
        not to lock you in!
Maybe it's, the same thing

**W**hat you seek is my approval…
        not my self.
So, it is more friendly
        that I turn you
        back to your self…
        the source
        of acceptance.
When you no longer need
        my approval…
I can give it to you.

You say you love me
because I understand you
better than you understand
yourself.

Sometimes, like now,
I wish I didn't
because it forces me to see
that it is also the reason
you will have to
leave me.

You slept on your own side of the bed
                last night....
It was a universe wide.
When I reached out to touch you
                all I could feel
                was the distance
                between.
It is still there today.
Your eyes... that soft bed blue...
                once my resting place...
are crowded with distant mountains
                and racing rivers.
And I'll be alone...
                with you...
                again tonight.

This is no carnival!
    I can ride with you…
    but,
    I am not
    your
    merry-go-round.
When you have discovered
    the difference…
I'll meet you at the Ferris wheel.

I don't smoke…

    so…

I never thought
    I would miss the stale smell
    of your bent,
    charred cigarretes
    on my bedside table.

    But,

    the clean ashtray
    was as glaring
    as a headlight,
    last night.

    I couldn't sleep.

If I smoked…

    maybe I wouldn't have noticed
    you were gone.

    Maybe.

Let me be angry...
      please.
      It is the only way
I can keep you from seeing
      how much
      I need you.

If I say "no" to you
>    I will lose you.
If I say "yes"…
>    I will lose myself.
Even if I win, I lose.
>    Or do I?

I am not a piece of jewelry
>to be worn
>so that others will admire you.
If you choose to continue…
>you must also remember
>that when jewelry is displayed
>…it can be stolen.

Will you try...just once,
        to be my age?
I'm tired of
        trying to be yours.

Stand up.
Let go of my hand.
Maybe then...
        I can let go of yours.
        You first.

**I** know you heard me…
but were you listening?

**B**etter stop now,
  before smiles become tightropes
  for words that step…
  with measured coolness…
across mechanical lips into deaf ear.

**P**lease get the hell out of my life…
        only…
            go softly…
            and don't let me see you go…
or I may call you back…
            and there is no one home.

**W**ait!
You can't leave me now.
What will I do with all these
                    Oreo cookies?

I warn you... I will not die of you.

I warn you... I will not die of you.

The silence is so loud,
I cannot hear my own advice.

Love, love... where are you?
You alone soothe the ache...
        and I cannot believe in you.

Today...
I know how lonely I am
      for you.
I have mistakenly called
      four people
      by your name.

The most I can hope for,
          right now,
is to make it to tomorrow…
          just once…
without listening
          for the phone.

I made the bed today.
I almost thought I was over you
                ... for a minute.

**I** never lied to you.
I always told you the truth
about love.

The joke is:
You listened to me.
I didn't.

# CHAPTER THREE

**I** crowed
What I knowed
Bestowed
What I knowed
You hoed
What I knowed
And growed
What I knowed
But I slowed
What I knowed
And stowed
What I knowed
Then you goed
Up the road
And I blowed
What I knowed.

I know myself...
Now that you have left...
    I shall be everywhere
      hoping to make such memories
        with someone else.
That is when I will really feel
      you have gone.

My body is suspended…
My mind is lost in space…
My tongue just wobbles loosely
                back and forth…
Saying nothing…
Doing nothing…
Out of time and out of place.
Like a bird…in dead of winter…
                flying north.

**W**hat were you…?
Who were you…?
Something in me…I know that.
        But you were like a drug.
While you were near,
        you were the ultimate "high."
With you…I could split atoms,
        stop time…
        stay young…
Or I thought I could.
But you only gave out small doses of yourself,
        enough to keep me coming back.
And I could never be sure
        when you would be available again.
Soooo…the inevitable crash…withdrawal!
I won't break windows, kill,
        or steal for a "fix"…
but I sometimes feel I might die
        for need of you.

As with tennis…
never play "Love"
with someone
whose game
is not as good as yours.
You'll end up losing…
and they won't
know enough
to care.

**W**ithout ever having you…
  I have lost you.
Without ever knowing you…
  I know you…
There is no history…
  Only a memory
  that never occurred at all.
  A memory…
  I can never forget.

It was a certain kind of sun, then…
And dreams and hopes hung like thick smoke
in the air.
Lyrics of songs jumped out at me
like playful kittens around
a corner.
It is a long-remembered, half-forgotten time.
Where is it now?
Waiting for me…or for you…somewhere?
Or has it gone its way…
like the morning of your smile?

We weren't living together,
                        anyway.
We were hiding together.

**"P**ain and loneliness make you strong…"
    I dish that one out a lot!
Today, I don't want to be strong.
    I want to dream just as much
    as anybody else.
But, I keep on paying my dues, anyway,
    and I really don't want
        to belong
        to that club
            anymore.

You were so busy finding yourself
in me...
That I had to run from you
To keep you from killing
both of us.

**H**ave you learned yet,
That who you know
      is not
        who you are?

The softer I walk
The louder I hear.

To own anything
          is to be owned by it.
I never wanted to own you....
          It's impossible....
And I never wanted to be owned.
But, I guess
          I always wanted you
          to pretend
          that you thought
          I was worth owning.

If all the "ifs" and "maybes,"
"wish-I-weres" and
          "could-have-beens-
          if-only-things-
          were-different-
          than-they-are"
could fall right off a cliff…
maybe I'd discover how
          to live with
          what is here and now…
but then,
I might as well forget this
          'cause I started it
                    with "if."

In those moments of despair…
        when I really don't care
        whether or not I survive,
then, am I most keenly aware
        of the certainty that I will.
                That's the pain of it…
                and the miracle.

# CHAPTER FOUR

**I** am astounded
at how long it takes
to discover...
for the first time,
the things I have learned...
over and over again
all my life.

The real growth
   is in recognizing
   that we do
   always get
what we want in life…
   one way or another.

**N**obody's perfect!
Somebody doesn't have to be.

**M**ost loneliness
is pain...
peering into mirrors
of self-pity
with the hope
of seeing someone else
to blame it on.

Listen to what you criticize
                    most severely
And you will hear
                    what you most fear
                    you are.

I was always afraid of
                risking *risk*.
But I found that I could stand
                to risk *risk*
better than I could stand
                to fear *fear*.
At least, risking
                brought about changes…
and the changes took up so much time,
I forgot what it was I was afraid
                to risk losing…
                in the first place.

The nicest thing about my life, now, is
that I am here with me
most of the time.

There is no such thing
      as perfect freedom...
There is only the freedom to
      discover
      that there is
no such thing
      as perfect freedom!

It is much easier to be lonely
without someone...
than it is to be lonely
with someone.

**R**eal belief
is a quiet thing...
too busy being itself
to look for disciples.

It is a waste of time and energy
　　　to worry about
　　　　　　what others are thinking
　　　　　　　　about you.

　　　　because...

You can never know
　　　exactly what another person
　　　　　　is thinking...AND,
　　　　　　the worst part it...
　　　they are usually not thinking
　　　　　about you at all.

They are too busy worrying about
　　　what others
　　　　　are thinking about them.

So, the truth is, all those terrible thoughts
　　　you thought they might
　　　　　be thinking about you,
　　　are your own thoughts
　　　　　about yourself.

Better spend your energy
    worrying about that...or,
        you just might
           convince somebody to think
what you were afraid
    they might be thinking
        after all.

It isn't always best
      to let everything
      spill out.
At times,
      there is more to be gained
      by using restraint!
Remember,
      it is the water
      held back by the dam
      that lights the city!

**A**lways trying
to be a good person
can be the biggest block
to becoming one.

To live happily with a pet,
one must first accept
      the responsibility
      of disciplining it
      consistently and firmly
      with much love!
To live happily with ourselves...
      it is the same.

**W**ho you are
is not
who you were...
It is who you are.

Any day of the week
I would choose to be "out"
          with others
          and in touch
          with myself...
than to be "in" with others
          and out of touch
          with myself.

I can tell how secure I am now.
I no longer clean the house
the day before the maid comes!

Love is not a thing
        to be "in" or "out" of.
It just is.
The beginning is the ending...
and the ending... the beginning...
Always and
        never...
        forever.

In youth...
        man seems to satisfy loneliness
                with passion....
And in maturity...
        aloneness...with compassion.
What a pity the difference
        is most often discovered
        after muscle and bone
        can no longer climb
            to the top
            of the mountain.

I have come to regard unrequited love
    like a hole in a sock.
    Mend it, or discard it!
Don't just stand there with cold feet!

Disciplining one's self
　　　　can be carried
　　　　too far.
It is alright to relax
　　　　part of the time.
Even the soils is richer
　　　　when it rests
　　　　every seven years.

If I keep talking about
        what I believe in…
Eventually…
        I will tell myself
        how much I believe in
        what I talk about.

Since I've finally
        taken responsibility
        for my life—
I can't tell you how often
        I've wanted
        to give it back.

But, nobody wants it.

Isn't that lucky?

Nothing matters, now.
I mean…
      everything matters so much
that nothing matters now.

**A**lone can be beautiful.
It's the one truth
      we know to be certain.
      We are
      *A Lone.*
To embrace that truth
      is the first step
      to becoming
      *Al One!*

# CHAPTER FIVE

**I** walk down another street.

Aware and alive
to the little I know,
as if I've arrived
at another plateau.
A plateau…familiar…
yet,
wonderfully strange
where I find my milieu
in the fortunes of change.

In my soul is a room
with a wedding inside….
Alone
is the groom
and Truth is
the bride.

Pity has gone
  to its place on a shelf…
  to be summoned for others
  but
  rarely for self.
    Touching and feeling
    in heart and in brain
    Accepting the healing
    of joy
    that's in pain….

Where *Alone* is not gloom,
  nor a fearsome divide.
    Alone is the groom
    and the Truth is
    the bride.

**Y**our alone-ness
      nourishes and protects
        my own.
I am always on the watch
      for you.
No need to wear a carnation!
I'll know you… by me…
        but you can hurry
        if you want to.

# EPILOGUE

I know you, by me…
      and me, by you.
A mirrored exchange
      of awareness…loving.
      Loving awareness…
            Always becoming…
            becoming always
            more you in me
            and me in you…
Growing separately together…
changing and remaining the same,
            eternally.

## ABOUT THE AUTHOR

Portia Nelson was a renaissance woman: author, singer, actress, composer, lyricist, painter, and photographer. She has appeared in such films as *The Sound of Music*, *Dr. Dolittle*, *The Trouble with Angels*, and *The Other*, as well as on the television soap opera *All My Children*, as Mrs. Gurney for many years. She performed on Broadway in the award-winning musical *The Golden Apple*.

Over the years she has written the music and lyrics for many revues, television specials, and films. Her song "Make a Rainbow" was sung by Marilyn Horne at President Clinton's inaugural ceremony.

As a singer, Ms. Nelson recorded five show albums for Columbia Records and three additional solo albums. She was also included in the Smithsonian collections *Cole Porter Songs* and *The American Popular Song*.

*There's a Hole in My Sidewalk* was made into a musical based on the book, and played at the York Theatre in Manhattan. Portia directed, wrote both the music and lyrics, and performed in the production.

*There's a Hole in My Sidewalk* was originally published in 1977 by Popular Library and was reprinted by the author in 1988. Since that time, the book has become a sought-after classic, but very hard to find. The poem "Autobiography in Five Short Chapters" has been reprinted in numerous publications. If you wish to use any of the material in this book, please contact the publisher.